Jessica Watson

Jessica Watson is an Australian sailor who gained international recognition in 2010 when she completed a solo circumnavigation of the world at the age of 16. She was born on May 18, 1993, in Queensland, Australia.

Watson's journey around the world began on October 18, 2009, and lasted for 210 days. She sailed approximately 23,000 nautical miles (42,600 kilometers) and crossed the equator twice during her voyage. Watson's journey was not without its challenges, and she faced numerous obstacles and setbacks, including being caught in a severe storm in the Southern Ocean.

After completing her journey, Watson received numerous accolades and awards, including being named the Young Australian of the Year in 2011. She has since become a motivational speaker, author, and advocate for environmental causes.

Jessica Watson's solo circumnavigation of the world made her the youngest person to ever complete such a journey, breaking the record previously held by Jesse Martin. Her accomplishment was widely celebrated in Australia and around the world, and she was awarded the Order of Australia Medal in recognition of her achievement.

Watson has continued to pursue her love of sailing, and has competed in a number of other ocean races and competitions. She has also written several books about her experiences, including her memoir "True Spirit: The Aussie girl who took on the world" and a children's book called "Indigo Blue".

In addition to her sailing career, Watson is also an advocate for environmental causes and is involved with a number of organizations working to protect the world's oceans. She has spoken about the impact of climate change on the ocean, and has emphasized the need for action to address this urgent issue.

Overall, Jessica Watson is a remarkable individual who has demonstrated incredible courage, determination, and resilience in pursuing her dreams and making a positive impact on the world.

Early life

Jessica Watson was born on May 18, 1993, in Queensland, Australia, and grew up on the Sunshine Coast. She developed a love of sailing at a young age, and began competing in local regattas when she was just eight years old.

Watson's parents were supportive of her passion for sailing, and they helped her buy her first boat when she was 11. She began sailing solo when she was 12, and quickly became an accomplished sailor. She also began dreaming of sailing around the world, and began preparing for such a journey when she was just 13 years old.

Watson's family was not wealthy, and she faced numerous challenges in raising the funds to finance her circumnavigation. However, she was determined to make her dream a reality, and worked tirelessly to secure sponsorships and support from the community.

Despite the challenges she faced, Watson remained focused and dedicated to her goal of circumnavigating the world. She spent countless hours training and preparing for the journey, and ultimately set sail on her historic voyage when she was just 16 years old.

Circumnavigation and publicity

Jessica Watson's solo circumnavigation of the world began on October 18, 2009, from Sydney Harbour, Australia. She sailed in her pink 34-foot yacht, which she named Ella's Pink Lady after her sponsor, the Pink Lady apple company.

Watson sailed across the Pacific Ocean, through the Panama Canal, across the Atlantic Ocean, around the Cape of Good Hope, and finally back to Sydney. Her journey lasted for 210 days, during which she sailed approximately 23,000 nautical miles (42,600 kilometers) and crossed the equator twice.

Watson's journey was not without its challenges. She faced severe storms, equipment failures, and other obstacles along the way. At one point, her yacht was hit by a 40-foot wave in the Southern Ocean, which caused significant damage to the boat. However, Watson remained calm and resourceful, and was able to make repairs and continue on her journey.

Watson's journey received significant media attention, both in Australia and around the world. She was interviewed by numerous media outlets, and her progress was closely followed by millions of people. Her achievement in completing a solo circumnavigation of the world at such a young age captured the public's imagination and inspired people around the world.

After completing her journey, Watson was greeted by thousands of well-wishers when she returned to Sydney Harbour on May 15, 2010. Her accomplishment was widely celebrated, and she received numerous accolades and awards, including being named the Young Australian of the Year in 2011.

Preparation

Jessica Watson spent several years preparing for her solo circumnavigation of the world, both physically and mentally. She underwent extensive training to prepare for the physical demands of the journey, and worked with a team of experts to make sure her yacht was equipped with the latest safety and navigation equipment.

Some of the steps she took to prepare for her journey include:

Physical training: Watson worked with a team of trainers and nutritionists to develop a fitness and nutrition plan that would help her stay healthy and strong during her journey. She spent countless hours training in the gym and on the water, and practiced various drills to prepare for emergencies.

Navigation and safety training: Watson worked with experienced navigators and sailors to improve her navigation and sailing skills. She learned how to use radar, GPS, and other navigation equipment, and practiced various safety drills to prepare for emergencies.

Boat preparation: Watson worked with a team of boat experts to make sure her yacht, Ella's Pink Lady, was in top condition for the journey. They made numerous upgrades and improvements to the boat, including adding a new navigation system and upgrading the safety equipment.

Mental preparation: Watson worked with a team of psychologists and mental health experts to prepare for the mental and emotional challenges of the journey. She practiced various techniques to manage stress and anxiety, and worked on developing a positive mindset.

Overall, Jessica Watson's preparation for her solo circumnavigation of the world was meticulous and thorough. Her dedication and hard work were key factors in her success in completing the journey.

Jessica Watson's boat for her solo circumnavigation of the world was a 34-foot (10.4-meter) yacht named Ella's Pink Lady. The boat was built in 1998, and was originally called Living Doll. Watson renamed the boat after securing a sponsorship from the Pink Lady apple company.

Ella's Pink Lady was a Sparkman & Stephens 34 design, and was equipped with the latest safety and navigation equipment. Some of the features of the boat include:

Watertight compartments: The boat had three watertight compartments, which helped prevent flooding in the event of a collision or other emergency.

Self-steering system: The boat was equipped with a self-steering system, which allowed Watson to take short breaks while the boat continued on course.

Emergency equipment: The boat was equipped with a variety of emergency equipment, including a life raft, flares, an emergency beacon, and a satellite phone.

Renewable energy: The boat had a solar panel and a wind turbine, which helped generate renewable energy to power the boat's electrical systems.

Upgrades and improvements: Watson and her team made numerous upgrades and improvements to the boat to make it more seaworthy and comfortable for the long journey.

Overall, Ella's Pink Lady was a sturdy and reliable boat that was well-suited for a solo circumnavigation of the world. Its performance and durability were key factors in Watson's successful completion of the journey.

Test run and collision

Before setting out on her solo circumnavigation of the world, Jessica Watson completed a number of test runs to prepare herself and her boat for the journey. One of the most significant test runs was a non-stop solo voyage from Sydney to Queensland and back, which she completed in early 2009.

During her test run, Watson faced a number of challenges, including rough seas, equipment failures, and sleep deprivation. However, she persevered and completed the journey successfully, which gave her confidence and experience for her upcoming circumnavigation.

However, a few months later, while she was still preparing for her circumnavigation, Ella's Pink Lady was involved in a collision with a 63,000-ton bulk carrier named Silver Yang off the coast of Moreton Bay in Queensland. The collision occurred while Watson was sailing the boat with an instructor as part of her training.

The collision caused significant damage to Ella's Pink Lady, including a broken mast and damaged rigging. Watson and her instructor were both shaken but unharmed. Watson's team worked around the clock to make repairs to the boat, and Watson was determined to continue with her circumnavigation as planned.

The collision raised questions about whether Watson was ready for such a challenging journey, and some critics suggested that she should abandon her circumnavigation attempt. However, Watson remained focused and determined, and ultimately completed her circumnavigation successfully, becoming the youngest person to sail solo around the world non-stop.

Journey

Jessica Watson's solo circumnavigation of the world began on October 18, 2009, when she departed from Sydney, Australia, in her yacht Ella's Pink Lady. She was just 16 years old at the time. Her goal was to become the youngest person to sail solo non-stop around the world.

Watson's journey took her through some of the most challenging waters in the world, including the Southern Ocean and the Tasman Sea. She faced numerous challenges along the way, including storms, equipment failures, and sleep deprivation. However, she remained focused and determined, and continued to make progress towards her goal.

One of the most challenging moments of Watson's journey came when she encountered a severe storm in the Southern Ocean, which generated waves up to 10 meters high. Watson managed to navigate the storm successfully and avoided serious damage to her boat.

After more than 200 days at sea, Watson returned to Sydney on May 15, 2010, completing her circumnavigation successfully. She became the youngest person to sail solo non-stop around the world, a record that she held until it was broken in 2012.

Throughout her journey, Watson was in regular contact with her family, friends, and supporters through a satellite phone and blog updates. Her journey captured the attention of people around the world, and she received numerous accolades and awards for her achievement.

Jessica Watson's solo circumnavigation of the world was a remarkable achievement, and demonstrated the determination, skill, and courage that are required to undertake such a challenging journey.

Ella's Pink Lady stays in
Queensland

After completing her solo circumnavigation of the world in 2010, Jessica Watson's yacht, Ella's Pink Lady, became a part of Queensland Maritime Museum's collection. The museum is located in Brisbane, Australia, and is dedicated to preserving Queensland's maritime history.

Ella's Pink Lady is now on display at the museum, where visitors can see the yacht up close and learn more about Watson's incredible journey. The yacht is a popular attraction at the museum, and has become an inspiration to many young people who dream of undertaking their own adventures.

Since arriving at the museum, Ella's Pink Lady has undergone extensive restoration work to ensure that it remains in good condition. The restoration work was carried out by a team of skilled craftsmen and volunteers, who worked to repair and replace damaged components and restore the yacht to its original condition.

In addition to being on display at the museum, Ella's Pink Lady is also used for educational purposes, with school groups and other visitors able to learn about sailing and maritime history through the yacht's story.

Overall, Ella's Pink Lady has become an important part of Queensland's maritime history, and a symbol of Jessica Watson's incredible achievement in completing a solo circumnavigation of the world at the age of just 16.

Criticism

Jessica Watson's solo circumnavigation of the world was not without criticism. Some questioned whether a 16-year-old girl had the experience and skills necessary to undertake such a challenging journey. Others suggested that Watson's journey was too risky and that she was putting herself in danger by attempting it.

In the lead-up to Watson's departure, there were calls for her to abandon her attempt, with some suggesting that her parents were putting her life in danger by allowing her to undertake the journey. There were also concerns about the financial cost of the journey, and some criticized Watson for accepting sponsorship from corporate sponsors.

After Watson completed her journey successfully, some continued to criticize her achievement, arguing that her voyage was not a true circumnavigation of the world because she did not cross the equator. Others suggested that Watson's record should not be recognized because she had stopped at ports during her journey to make repairs.

Despite the criticism, Watson remained focused on her goal and completed her journey successfully. She also used her journey as an opportunity to raise awareness about the importance of pursuing one's dreams and the need to take calculated risks in life.

Overall, while Watson's solo circumnavigation of the world was not without controversy, it remains a remarkable achievement and a testament to her determination and courage.

Praise

Jessica Watson's solo circumnavigation of the world received widespread praise and recognition, both in Australia and around the world. Many people admired her determination, courage, and skill in undertaking such a challenging journey at such a young age.

Watson's achievement inspired people around the world, particularly young people, to pursue their dreams and to never give up, even when faced with adversity. She became a role model for many, and her story showed that anything is possible if you set your mind to it.

Watson received numerous accolades and awards for her achievement, including being named Young Australian of the Year in 2011. She also received the Medal of the Order of Australia and was inducted into the Australian National Maritime Museum's Hall of Fame.

In addition to the recognition she received for her solo circumnavigation, Watson has also been praised for her charitable work and advocacy on behalf of young people. She has used her platform to raise awareness about issues such as mental health and education, and has worked to inspire young people to pursue their passions and make a positive difference in the world.

Overall, Jessica Watson's solo circumnavigation of the world was a remarkable achievement that earned her widespread praise and recognition. She demonstrated that with hard work, determination, and perseverance, anything is possible.

Awards

Jessica Watson received numerous awards and accolades for her solo circumnavigation of the world, including:

Young Australian of the Year: Watson was named Young Australian of the Year in 2011, in recognition of her achievement in completing a solo circumnavigation of the world at the age of 16.

Medal of the Order of Australia: Watson was awarded the Medal of the Order of Australia in 2011, in recognition of her service to sailing and to the community.

Australian Geographic Society's Young Adventurer of the Year: Watson was named the Australian Geographic Society's Young Adventurer of the Year in 2010, in recognition of her achievement in completing a solo circumnavigation of the world.

International Association of Cape Horners' Special Recognition Award: Watson received the International Association of Cape Horners' Special Recognition Award in 2010, in recognition of her achievement in completing a solo circumnavigation of the world.

Inaugural recipient of the Spirit of Adventure Award: Watson was the inaugural recipient of the Spirit of Adventure Award, which was presented to her by the Governor-General of Australia in 2010.

In addition to these awards, Watson was also inducted into the Australian National Maritime Museum's Hall of Fame, and has received numerous other honors and recognitions for her achievement.

Further projects

After completing her solo circumnavigation of the world, Jessica Watson continued to pursue her passion for sailing and embarked on several other projects and initiatives.

In 2012, Watson sailed as part of the crew of the Sydney to Hobart Yacht Race, one of the world's most challenging ocean races. She also worked as a crew member on various other sailing projects and initiatives, including the Australian Youth Climate Coalition's 2013 Pacific Climate Warriors campaign.

In addition to her sailing pursuits, Watson has also been involved in a number of charitable and advocacy initiatives. She has worked as an ambassador for the Australia Day Council, and has been involved in programs aimed at promoting youth leadership and engagement.

Watson has also written several books, including her memoir "True Spirit: The True Story of a 16-Year-Old Australian Who Sailed Solo, Nonstop, and Unassisted Around the World", which was published in 2010. She has also written a children's book, "Poppy and the Wind", which was published in 2014.

Overall, Jessica Watson has continued to inspire and motivate people around the world with her passion for sailing, her advocacy work, and her commitment to making a positive difference in the world.

In popular culture

Jessica Watson's solo circumnavigation of the world captured the attention of the media and the public, and her story has been portrayed in various forms in popular culture.

Documentary films: Several documentaries have been made about Watson's journey, including "210 Days: Around the World with Jessica Watson" (2010) and "Jessica Watson: The True Story" (2012).

Books: In addition to Watson's own memoir, several books have been written about her journey, including "Solo: One Girl's Story of Survival" by Jacki French (2011) and "Jessica's Journey" by Kristin Weidenbach (2012).

Film adaptation: In 2018, it was announced that a film adaptation of Watson's journey was in development, with production expected to begin in 2020.

Printed in Great Britain
by Amazon

23143571R00030